CHARGED, CHALLENGED AND CHANGED!!!

When do we win? "When we believe we can"

KENNY MARSHBURN

Copyright © 2016 by Kenny Marshburn

Charged, Challenged And Changed!!!
When do we win? "When we believe we can"
by Kenny Marshburn

Printed in the United States of America.

ISBN 9781498486583

All rights reserved solely by the author. The author guarantees all contents are original and do not infringe upon the legal rights of any other person or work. No part of this book may be reproduced in any form without the permission of the author. The views expressed in this book are not necessarily those of the publisher.

Unless otherwise indicated, Scripture quotations are taken from the King James Version (KJV) – public domain

www.xulonpress.com

Introduction

One of the most life charging, challenging and changing things that ever happened to me was nasal pharynx cancer.

The tumor was so close to the memory area of my brain that they could not remove it. The doctors offered nothing positive, only chemotherapy and forty straight days of radiation along with a stomach tube and the removal of eighteen lymph nodes from my neck. At the very onset of this horrendous life-claiming physical dilemma, of all people to give the greatest encouragement to begin my fight for life was my fourteen-year-old son, Cody. He came through and power boosted my faith that all would turn out well—in a most unusual way.

I knew that I could not bring the news of my diagnosis to my two boys without breaking into tears. The thought of leaving my wife and two sons was a bit much, to say the least. So, I had my pastor come to my home to inform them of my circumstance.

Standing before our fireplace, there in the living room, Pastor Huntley did a superb job of breaking the news to my Carson and Cody about their dad's cancer situation.

When he was finished, Cody spoke up and asked very bluntly, "Is my dad going to die?"

All of a sudden out of nowhere, I just spoke out loud, "*Absolutely not!*"

My boy wanted an answer to a very serious question, however, when the question left his mouth and entered my ears, I felt an instant challenge wash all over me.

Cody turned and went to his bedroom and resumed doing whatever it was he was doing, knowing that Dad was going to be fine *after the fight.*

Dear reader, are you in a fight, a struggle, or a standstill?

It may not be physical, however roadblocks and obstacles are pouring in like a flood: overwhelming odds, problems, pressure, and predicaments; troubles, trials and tribulations.

Are you going to die?

Absolutely not!

Join me on a three step revelatory and refreshing journey to charge, challenge and change!

Chapter One
Charge

"A DIRECTION PERCEPTION"

Personally, I feel direction, in many cases, can be more instrumental in your charge than power. For example, lightning is more powerful than 120 volts, but because lightning has no specific direction, it becomes hazardous rather than helpful.

It's much like dreaming. Dreams are great when they don't become nightmares. Dream the dream, plan the plan, and then be sure to develop specific direction. Remember: a plan will not work if you do not work your plan. Also, dreams come true for those who don't oversleep.

In Psalm 30:5, David said, "Weeping may endure for the night, but joy cometh in the morning."

Someone else said, "When is the morning?"

Then it came to me in my dilemma with cancer: the morning comes when you *wake up*!

We are giants in our day because we carry the greatest message ever told: the gospel of Jesus Christ. Do not think for one moment the enemy of our souls will take that lying down. Well, neither should we.

It's a good thing to "be the lightning bolt" that jolts everyone around us into excitement and enthusiasm; however, a good game plan will create the continuum that all of us need to finish; so, along with power: *plan*!

"BEYOND THE THOUGHT PROCESS"

I'm not speaking of simple positive thinking. Positive thinking certainly has its merit, but to only think it will not accomplish it. You may be thinking, *I think positive; however, my personality and my demeanor are not positive*. Even so, this writer believes every one of us wants to be the one who fires it up and gets things initiated and moving.

So, charge! Get up and *go*! In Matthew 28:19, Jesus said, "*Go*." Nothing is stopping us; we have permission granted to us by God. We are not simply overcomers; "we are more than conquerors through Him who loves us" (Romans 8:37).

When He said, "Go," He then said, "into all the world." That means you can lead, overcome, conquer, and accomplish in any area or situation in your world. It also helps to know He said He would be with us all the days of our lives (Matthew 28:20).

A whole book in the New Testament was committed to action. The book of Acts is that: the actions of the Apostles. Thank you Jesus for the thoughts that you poured into those faithful few. Where would the New Testament church be today if the Apostles and disciples of Jesus Christ had not put the words and thoughts and the plans and dreams of the Savior into *action*?

You be the one that stands up, motivates and ushers in an atmosphere filled with energy. Feel the charge to start. Then, no matter how long it takes, *finish* what you started so others can follow your footsteps to a better future.

"DELIVERANCE ATTITUDE"

Ok, you may be asking *How do I become that person?*

First of all you must know that you do not have to be the one who has all the answers to all of life's issues. However, we can be the one that says, *Hey, let's put some heads and hearts together here.* The answer, the solution, the hope and the help we need is right here with us and in us.

I was a complete stranger to cancer treatments, chemo, radiation and all of that. On my first day of treatment on October fifth, my wife and I arrived at the cancer center on the third floor at 10:00 a.m. An IV was placed into the back of my right hand to allow the chemo to flow: Cisplatin at

100 milligrams (very high dose). I will never forget it. After IV preparation and just before chemo, I stepped out into the hallway waiting room, and there was my pastor, Wayne Huntley, two of my dearest friends and pastors, Dennis Landtroop and Scott Smith, along with one of the humblest men of God I know to this day, Wayne McLane. I was so surprised, I cried; I couldn't help it. I weep even now as I write. My wife, my friends and my pastor, all there to help me with the charge I needed to face my future with great faith.

After a brief time and faith-filled prayer with these fine folks, I made my way to the little chapel on the second floor of the hospital, and there I met with my savior, my king, my everything.

When I left that little chapel on the second floor, I felt that I could have charged hell with a cup of ice water. With the faith and encouragement from my wonderful wife and friends, and then to top it off in the presence of the Lord, I felt as if that was all I needed to charge into the unknown, untold and uncertain future.

Isaiah said, "Come now, and let us reason together" (Isaiah 1:18). Together we can initiate the effort to resolve any situation at any given time, and anywhere, with the presence and the promise of our God.

I've always said attitude determines altitude. Mentally and spiritually, we can fly as high or as low as we choose. So lose the puppy dog "don't know what to do" look, even when you don't know what to do. I'm not saying, "Fake it till you make it." That philosophy frightens me. Number one, it sounds too hypocritical, and number two, I feel if I fake it, I'll never make it. Life-threatening obstacles are real and they come at you full throttle. Pretending they don't is dangerous to mind, body and soul.

Ask yourself, *What's wrong with being the one who's willing to crash the pity party and charge the situation with grit, gut and determination?* Charge after every difficulty, Stand up declaring ultimate victory and present arms. Lift the sword of the spirit (Ephesians 6:17). Things may be really bad, but the answer is on the way, and the answer will be sweeter than the bitterness of the dilemma.

Don't forget, we are not just conquerors. We are more than conquerors (Romans 8:37).

You've got more charge than you may even know. Remember, if you have God's heart, he's got your back.

"THE ELEMENT OF SURPRISE"

When I woke up from what was supposed to be a simple one-tonsil removal, I noticed my wife's tears. Surprised? Absolutely, to say the least, but in a flash I redirected and looked deep into her eyes and said, "I have cancer, don't I?"

She broke into a deep sob and said, "Yes."

I took her by the hand and said, "At least I know where my battle is."

I didn't know what I was going to have to go through to get over cancer, especially with it being found in the nasal cavity area. It was so close to my throat region and brain stem that they couldn't surgically remove the tumor.

That very moment, I began my fight. Cancer may have come against me, but I became determined, that, sink or swim, live or die, I was coming against cancer.

You probably know the story of David's miracle with the Giant in 1 Samuel Chapter 17, but let me refresh your memory. A shepherd boy, probably between the ages of twelve and sixteen had to defeat a giant who was about 9 feet tall, his spear weighing in at about sixty-five pounds. David beat the giant incidentally. But, I didn't even have a slingshot. Or what about Shamgars' ox goad? In Judges 3:31, an ox goad is nothing more than a stick used to prod cattle along. He slew six hundred Philistines with it. But I didn't have an ox goad. I didn't even have Gideon's pitcher; they won that battle without firing a shot (Judges 7:20). Weapons that were outdated and unusual perhaps, but at least they had them.

I'm sorry, my friend, but hope is not enough. You have got to summon the warrior within.

Paul told Timothy to stir up the gift that is within you (2 Timothy 1:6). God has given us the spirit of love, power and a sound mind.

I found my slingshot, my ox goad and my pitcher, when I realized that according to Isaiah 54:17, no weapon that is formed against me shall prosper; every tongue that shall rise against me in judgment thou shalt condemn. This is the heritage of the servants of the lord, and their righteousness is of me, saith the Lord.

All the way from your salvation to your situation, you have had overcoming power flowing through your veins and traveling right beside you.

"YOU MUST NOT FORGET"

"Greater is he that is within you, than he that is in this world" (1 John 4:4).

"Rejoice not against me oh mine enemies, for when I fall, I shall arise; when I sit in darkness, the Lord shall be a light unto me" (Micah 7:8).

You are not going to lose it. Why? Because you are going to use it.

Your dilemma is going to release hidden strengths and great faith at greater levels and dimensions of courage.

It's ok to be the deer in the headlights occasionally. Just don't stand there too long; there's a vehicle behind the headlights.

"FIGHT NOT FLIGHT"

We can all be purpose driven, until we come against an opposition that is bigger than our purpose. Then, my friend, you need authority.

In the scripture I Timothy 6:12, fight came before faith. However, where there is no faith there is no fight.

All of us come to the edge of "get up or give up" sooner or later—usually a whole lot sooner than later. We must accept our destiny, express no fear and *charge* into the future, sometimes with nothing except faith-filled expectations.

Lying in the hospital during chemo and radiation, I came to that place. All of a sudden, about midnight, a nurse stepped into my room. She kindly asked, "Mr. Marshburn, how do you feel?"

Wrong time for that question, because God as my witness, I felt I would not make it until the sunrise. "I'm not doing very well at all. I feel as if I'm slowly slipping away." It was really bad; I couldn't move, I laid on my back with hands folded on my chest, with the Devil whispering to me, "This is the way you will look in your casket."

Now take in mind, I've never seen this nurse before that night, I never saw her again after that night, but what she said before she stepped out of my hospital room could have been what got the ball rolling toward saving my life.

She was pushing her hand against the door to leave when she turned and looked directly at me, "I heard you are a preacher?"

I politely replied yes.

"Then why don't you try some of that stuff you preach?"

My first reaction was, "What the what?" And before I could even respond to her statement, the door closed and she was gone.

I continued to run what the nurse said through my mind: *try the stuff you preach.*

Lying there, the only thing I could move was my right index finger, but my voice was not limited. At that moment, a chorus came to mind; I couldn't remember all the words, but I did remember that it said, "This is how we overcome." I began singing that. I kept the rhythm with my index finger against my chest. Over and over I softly sang, "this is how we overcome, this is how we overcome, this is how we overcome." My hand started moving, I kept singing, and suddenly I could raise my hand in praise. I continued to sing. The strength came to me to sit up. Still singing, "this is how we over come," I turned and swung my legs off the bed. I would not stop singing, because I knew a miracle was unfolding right before my very eyes. I stood up, and with all the med hookups, tubes and connections, I began pacing. Still singing. And with his peace that passes all understanding, he washed all over me in my worship.

The situation became very clear: I will not die tonight. *Absolutely not!*

My journey to charge, challenge and change was not nearly over, but I began to understand that when you're down, you can still stand (Romans 8:28).

We know that all things work together for good for those who love God and are called according to his purpose. The question is not, what is my dilemma, but rather, what is my song?

Choose your own battle hymn, and *charge*.

The future is worth the fight. Stay in the faith, follow the father, and never give up!

Continue with me here, and do not let the Devil steal your next level.

Chapter Two
Challenge

"THAT'S A GOOD START"

During the intervals of hospital stays for chemotherapy and radiation treatments, not to mention draining tubes, feeding tubes and surgeries, prayer became a constant and comforting companion. During this time, I also felt a need to call a prophet and great man of God, T.W. Barnes. I shared my cancer dilemma story with him, and also about how much I was praying and reaching out to God. Just like the nurse I mentioned earlier, he challenged my charge with his unexpected answer. I expected his reply to be something along the lines of, "that's great, exactly what God wants", "perfect", or at least, "good job."

Instead, Brother Barnes reply was simply, "that's a good start." How true it was. The man of God sensed it. I needed more than simple gratitude for a job well done. I needed to prepare for the journey to charge, challenge and change. And for me, it had just begun.

My wife's tears, the nurse's mini sermon and TW Barnes's revelation all culminated into a charge and challenge to forge into the future, as long as my future was there.

"DOWN IS THE NEW UP"

Simply put, I believe that we all stand tallest when we are on our knees.

Here are three points to ponder in reference to prayer when you are feeling challenged:

- When you pray you stay.

Prayers create stayers, the race is not given to the swiftest; it is given to the one that endures until the end (Ecclesiastes 9:11). Prayer should never be simply something we try. Prayer should be something we live, love, and give, non-stop.

- When we weep, we reap.

Matthew 5:4: *blessed* are they that mourn for they shall be comforted.

God loves to mend the broken, so cry out from your personal prayer space and unleash the tender mercies of a God that delights in meeting the needs of his children. The answer may not come right when you want it, but it will always be on time.

In Psalms 34:4, David said, "I sought the Lord, and he heard me, and delivered me from all my fears."

- Humility will always get you an appointment with the King.

James 4:6 tells us God gives grace unto the humble.

During my cancer battle, prayer was my keeping force. I was never too weak to pray, nor did I feel such pity for myself that I could not pray.

Prayer is the fuel that flies our needs to the throne. We must never give up on prayer.

"WHAT TIME IS IT?"

All of us have metal, substance, and fortitude within. Finding it will charge us onward into our destiny. That, and remembering without a doubt, that, "Greater is he that is in you, than he that is in the world" (1 John 4:4).

I came through the charge. Now, it was *time* for the challenge!

I sincerely hope the story of my time and experience with cancer teaches you and that no form of cancer ever reaches you.

I write to you while in flight on a ministry trip from Michigan to my home state of North Carolina with tears in my eyes. The words that I write to you bring back afresh the flood of emotion and suffering my little family and I went through during that dreadful fight for life. My dear friend, cancer is very bad. If you know of anyone in that crisis, please do not let them walk that walk alone. You do not have to have answers or be able to resolve all of life's troubles. Just be there with care, concern and companionship. Love, thoughtfulness and friendship are like tuna fish; a little portion can go a long way.

The memory of the pain and suffering, the agony and humiliation that I went through, I would not wish that experience on my most terrible enemy. However, what God gave me, where he took me and how he was a constant comfort and companion cannot be put into words; that part of the experience is not for sale at any price.

"I RAN, BUT THERE WAS NO PLACE TO HIDE"

I came up in a home with seven children. My age placed me in the middle. Many times during childhood squabbles, it was fight or flight. I did not coin the phrase that says, "you can run, but you cannot hide", but I could have easily. Actually the phrase is attributed to Joe Lewis in 1946 on the evening of his fight with the light heavyweight champion Billy Conn.

Champions are not born, they are forged by challenge.

Every fight may not produce the same winner. However, that fact has never stopped winners from accepting the fight.

Not all of us can "float like butterflies and sting like bees" (Mohammed Ali) however; all of us can fight a good fight, keep the faith and achieve an incorruptible crown on that great day of the Lord's appearing.

Paul the Apostle of Jesus Christ said, " I fought a good fight, I have finished my course, I have kept the faith: Henceforth there is laid up for me a crown of righteousness, which the Lord, the righteous judge, shall give me at that day: and not to me only, but unto all them also that love his appearing" (2 Timothy 4:7-8).

Another good thing to take note of and to remember is that either way, one way or another, *we win*! Because Paul also said, "For me to live is Christ, and to die is gain" (Philippians 1:21). The man was a spiritual kamikaze for Christ.

List the things worth fighting for. Accept the challenge and face your giant.

"WE HAVE THE ROCK"

According to historians, Goliath's spear weighed over sixty pounds, but God had the situation under control from the very beginning when Goliath challenged Israel. David's rock created the universe—not the rock in his hand, but the rock in his heart.

David told Goliath in 1 Samuel 17:45, "You come to me with a sword, with a spear, and with a javelin. But I come to you in the name of the Lord of hosts."

My attitude is, "On Christ the solid rock I stand, all other ground is sinking sand.

He's my rock, my sword, my shield, my protector, my guide and my God."

Somewhere, sooner or later, we have to face our fight. Accept the challenge and charge into change. Take dominion and be led into new adventures and frontiers in Christ. If you do not become the lead dog, I can promise the scenery will never change.

There are choices to be made when we are challenged. Hebrews 11:6 says, "Our God is a rewarded of those that diligently seek him."

If we are not obedient to the rewarder, then our faith is in the devourer. The rewarder (Jesus Christ) came to seek and to save (Luke 19:10). The devourer (Satan) came to seek and destroy. (John 10:10). Wherein lies our loyalty, in the rock or the reject?

"OUR SOURCE OF STRENGTH"

Nehemiah 8:10 says, "the joy of the Lord is your strength." Pardon the vernacular, but that's why it is a mandate from hell for us not to praise our God, because praise exalts the Lord and he in turn gives us strength.

The Lord inhabits (lives within) our praise (Psalms 22:3). Adoration, worship and praise from his people brings God great joy. Note, the joy of the Lord is your strength. So, if I bring him joy, he in turn has promised me strength. Praise him out of your past; praise him in your present and praise into your future.

Life is going to happen. We need a plan that works, then we need to work our plan.

Praise raised this writer off of my deathbed and carried me from doom and gloom all the way to the throne room. There in the presence of God, I obtained mercy, grace and strength in my struggle.

Since that time I made a solemn vow to my redeemer. I told God that if he doesn't want me to praise him, he will have to kill me. I will go to my grave giving him the praise he is so worthy of.

A very interesting point is that there are no qualifications for praise. The Bible says in Psalms 150:6, "Let everything that hath breath praise the Lord."

Release your heartfelt praise on him. It will bring him great joy, no matter who you are. And then the strength will begin to flow. When God becomes your priority, your problems become his property. And whatever pleases God freezes the Devil. Let the joy of the Lord be your strength.

"AGREE WITH THE DECREE"

God's Word is a sacred decree. It is a promise. His word shall never pass away (Matthew 24:35). The Word of God is true, it is right and it is settled. I promise, your prayer is heard, it is important and it will be answered. Don't let doubt cause you to miss out. Respond to the Word and the promises of God in a positive manner. Stand up and stand out. All the promises of God are yea and amen. God's promises belong to you. Believe it and let that settle it.

Create a confident relationship in God's Word. The Bible is not a coffee table book; it's life and it is real. Are we lacking in relationship with our God if we remain illiterate in His Word? David said, "Thy word have I hid in mine heart, that I might not sin against thee" (Psalms 119:11).

This is your turning point. Power, authority and dominion await you in the arena of change.

"DIRTY THINGS"

In John Chapter 8, they brought a woman to Jesus to be stoned. They accused her of dirty things. Jesus began to scribble around in the dirt. Did he write their names and list the dirty things they did? Was he reminded of where all men had their origin (Genesis 2:7)? Was he thinking about where all flesh would go back? Is that why he said, "Let him that is without sin cast the first stone"? Why would the dirty want to stone the dirty?

It doesn't matter how dirty you think you are, or how dirty you think you're not. Christ died for all of us. There is just as much mercy, grace, healing and help for you and me as there is for anyone else in this world.

Jesus's grace is our replacement for being complacent. The master would heal you, cleanse you and set you free. He has set the open door of change before you that no man can shut, but that any man can open.

Just as Elisha of old, the Lord has sent an unworthy servant to tell you that your Jordan awaits. You can be cleansed, restored, renewed and refreshed. Regardless of what your circumstances are, it is your chance for change, because this great privilege and opportunity comes to us all (Ecclesiastes 9:11).

I know, because he saved me, physically, mentally and spiritually. And what he's done for me, he will take great joy and pleasure in doing for you.

The little boy stood over the dry and thirsty flower with a big cup of water. He spoke to the flower and said, "I have the power of life or death over you, I can give you this water and let you live, or I can just walk away and let you die." The little boy decided to walk away with the water and let the flower die. Suddenly, it began to rain.

Whatever you are facing or feeling, turn it over to Jesus and let it rain.

Change is coming.

Chapter Three

Change

"I CAN DO THIS"

During my fight with cancer, chemo, feeding tubes, radiation and medication, my faithful wife, Evelyn, kept a journal. She must have filled two or three legal pads with day-to-day step-by-step procedures and events. I wish to share one of those events recorded on October 7th:

> 11:15 a.m., the nurse checked Kenny's blood pressure 146/82. 12:50, pain and nausea severe vomiting. He was given meds for pain and nausea at 1:00 p.m. 3:30 p.m., nausea. medication given. I gave him a sponge bath, helped him put on his pajamas and a clean t-shirt. He has fallen asleep. It's 6:00 p.m. and he's still sleeping. Thank you Jesus, you are

Change

so awesome. At 6:45, He woke up severely sick, given nausea medication at 6:45pm. He is sitting on side of bed. 7:00 p.m. pain medicine through IV. Pain above his eyes. It's now 12 midnight, Ativan for nausea, Morphine for pain. Kenny became extremely sick again. He is vomiting and saying, "Evelyn, it's not that bad really, it's not that bad. I can do this."

"As for me, I will call upon God; and the Lord shall save me. Evening and morning, and at noon, will I pray, and cry aloud: and he shall hear my voice. He hath delivered my soul in peace from the battle that was against me: for there were many with me" *(Psalm 55:16-18)*.

"GOD GETS IN THE WAY"

It was just one of those crazy things you feel, not often enough to be annoying, but enough not to ignore. It had to be God. I felt it so strong I could not just let it go. The Lord said, "You need to go to Wal-Mart." Again the impulse was so strong that there was nothing to do but go to Wal-Mart. So, I went. I was walking past the pharmacy area when all of a sudden I came face-to-face with the reason for the crazy, sudden impulse and voice of God. A gentleman out of nowhere turned the corner of the aisle and we were eye-to-eye. I saw the metal staples on the side of his neck, the pale look on his face, the eyes familiarly hollow from long sessions of chemo and radiation. *Oh mercy Lord, he's going through what I went through.* I spoke first. I said, "Sir I see you are in a battle. I just came out of the same situation."

All of a sudden, he lit up with the expression of, *finally, someone that understands and knows what I'm going through.* I went on to tell him I'm finished with the treatments and the results are, no cancer. My next words were just as encouraging to me as they were to him. I told him God is the only one that heals from cancer, and he healed me. God does not love one person more than another; what he did for me he will gladly do for you.

He began to weep. With words choked by sobbing he said, "I was sitting at home becoming more depressed by the minute, then I felt an urge to just get out and go somewhere, then I wound up here."

After a short testimony and a few words of encouragement, we prayed together. He left cheerful, smiling and full of faith. He and his good wife could not thank me enough for being there, right on time. I could not thank God enough for using me to lead someone toward help, hope and great faith in the One that heals. It was a great wonder to watch God get in the way of depression, sickness and hopelessness.

In Genesis 22, The Binding of Isaac is an interesting subject to me. In Hebrew the *Akedát,* also known as "The Binding", is a story from the Hebrew Bible in which God asks Abraham to sacrifice his son, Isaac, on Mount Moriah.

The account states that Abraham bound Isaac, his son, before placing him on the altar. Keep that in mind there are three things that are of the utmost certainty: Jesus is the truth, the life and the way (John 14:6).

I rebuke and come against anything that would try to convince you that the Lord would hinder, block or get in the way of your joy, happiness or good fortune:
- He is our joy
- He is our happiness
- He is our fortune

Gods not hindering, he's helping. He's not hurting; he's healing.

Gods not holding us back, he's got our back.

Isaac carried the wood for his own sacrifice to Mt. Moriah. He and his dad were bent on getting Isaac dead. But what happened? God got in the way.

I may be speaking to people hell bent on their own destruction, but God is making preparations to get in your way. *Isaac, no way out of this son, it's a done deal. You are going to die today.* And then, God got in the way.

Guilt may have you so bound that you feel as if you are packing your own wood for your burning.

Go ahead Isaac, put yourself on the altar and watch God get right in the way of death and destruction.

We must always remember, heaven wasn't made for the Devil, and hell wasn't made for you. Accept and believe in a better tomorrow. Tomorrow is coming; it may as well be better.

God will never tempt one to do evil, but he will tempt us to do good. Abraham passed the test. He obeyed his God, and then God got in the way.

In Genesis 22:13 the Lord prepared a ram, and Isaac was set free by the ram. In Luke 2:11 he provided a lamb. We have been set free by the lamb. He is a savior and a friend who will stick closer than a brother.

Let God get in the way.

"LEAD"

The master has chosen men, women and young people who, in many cases, were a mess, just like you and I perhaps in our pasts. However, they created testimonies of his saving grace and saving messages for all mankind.

We must rise to the forefront and become living, breathing testimonials of the healing and saving grace of God. I firmly believe we will turn our nation around in great refreshing and revival. This is something we need so desperately from our house to the White House.

This dynamic team of encouragers, motivators and campaigners for Christ desperately needs strong-willed and Christ-minded leadership—one of them may as well be you.

Your family, church and nation need *you*.

Many Americans are either numb or in limbo about what's happening in our country. Quality in public schools is spiraling downhill. Teachers are giving up. History, regarding the price paid for life, liberty and freedom for all, is being blatantly ignored. America needs Bible-believing Christian leaders—great people, just like yourself, who have accepted the charge, the challenge and the change to do great exploits and to believe God for the impossible.

Our hidden vices and addictions must be sacrificed on a true altar of repentance so we can advance in our ministry and missions. Our God is able. Ephesians 3:20-21, "Now unto Him who is able to do exceedingly abundantly above all that we ask or think, according to the power that works in us, to Him *be* glory in the church by Christ Jesus to all generations, forever and ever." Amen.

There are blessings in bad times. Matthew 5:4, says, "*Blessed* are they that mourn for they shall be comforted."

When we are moved with passion, we mourn. When we mourn, God gives us assistance so that we can stand up. When we stand up, we make a difference, and then, we change our world. I don't want to make as much sense as I do a difference. As children of God, we are the people with the peace that passes all understanding. "And the peace of God, which passeth all understanding, shall keep your hearts and minds through Christ Jesus" (Philippians 4:7).

"LOSSES AND CROSSES"

There's a huge difference between standing out and being set apart. People set apart are people pulled from the crowd, and changed.

George Guy said, "Character is developed in our deepest trials. The measuring stick of God is never placed on us on our mountaintops. It's always in our valleys."

Character is a distinguishing quality of ethical traits that set you aside from the norm. Your character is something that comes naturally without effort.

Spending too long on the mountaintop has a tendency to make us prideful and forgetful about the trials and suffering that others are going through. Always remember that your soul is only restored in the valley. Valleys are where green pastures are found and places of still waters. Your reaction to your losses and crosses (burdens) will determine your character, spiritual growth, and your victories.

The opinions we have formed in our minds about Job did not take place when he was a millionaire. They were put in our minds in the darkest hours of his trials.

What we consider our losses and crosses define us more than our victories.

"DON'T DIE IN A DILEMMA"

There was a Sunday night toward the end of my ordeal with cancer that I wanted to be in church so desperately. My wife wrote about it in her journal:

> Sunday night, Kenny really wanted to go to church. He was so very weak. As I was helping him to get ready, he became very sick. We finished getting ready and went to church. He was only able to stay about thirty-five minutes until we had to come back home. We were up all through the night with Kenny trying to clear his throat. He choked and gagged many times. He threw up as well. I feel that when he gets a week or so past having radiation, that this will get better. Since we came home from Kenny's last hospital stay, he has thrown up each day, mostly in the mornings when he struggles to clear his throat. He does pretty well with the new food, water and medicines most of the time. I'm sure the pain patch has helped greatly with relieving some of his pain. Plus, I know our biggest resource has been *God*.

It's now Monday, back to radiation. Five more treatments and radiation will be over.

I thank God for my wonderful wife and a tremendous church family that walked with me and supported me with so much strength and passion. In times like that, isolation is a sure trip to annihilation. I am not so proud that I will not admit, I cannot succeed on my own, and there is no doubt that we all have a common enemy—one that will take a team effort to overcome.

As a cancer victim, I do not deny that I had a serious dilemma. But I refused to let the dilemma have me.

"GRACE"

Paul wrote over half the New Testament, and the same Paul passed his mentors up in ministry. He has a thorn. No one knows exactly what the thorn was. Speculation says it was something physical.

When he prayed for his thorn to be removed, the Lord replied with this answer: "My grace is sufficient."

The fact that the Lord brought up the subject of grace led me to believe it was a conscience thing that tormented Paul.

Think with me for a moment. Before Paul received the revelation of who Jesus was on the road to Damascus, he was in the process of totally destroying Christian lives. He imprisoned them, it was even recorded that he held their coats while an angry anti-Christian mob stoned Stephen to death, a devoted follower of Christ. Who knows how many Christian martyrs Paul was involved with or consented to.

The memory alone must have caused so much guilt that Paul, this born again, great man of God, felt he could not bear it.

Why else would the Lord say, "My grace is enough"?

My friend, we are charged, challenged and the best part, *we are changed* by the blood of Jesus Christ.

The Spirit of God spoke to Paul and forgave him.

Paul, you may have a ton of memory, but the Lord was saying, "I have sufficient mercy."

Change is the greatest challenge in life, however, no matter how difficult change can be, it is still a very vital part of successful living. Believe and receive the change.

It's ok to remember past struggles, troubles and dirty deeds as long as our past remains a testimony of the saving grace of God and the delivering hand of a holy savior.

Paul's past wrote hope for all of mankind to see. There is no sinner so bad, no deed so dastardly that my God's grace is not sufficient enough to wash away, cleanse and set apart for his purpose.

Today is the day; we walk away from past regrets and the heaviness of guilt.

There is no condemnation to those who are in Christ Jesus. Celebrate the new life.

Can you even begin to fathom what great, powerful and awe-inspiring things lie ahead when we simply accept the charge and challenge to move forward out of darkness and into his marvelous light (1Peter 2:9)?

"I'VE GOT YOU COVERED"

The lamb had to bleed, so his spirit could lead.
The children of Israel left Egypt filled with the lamb and covered by the blood.
In one night, the Israelites were changed, from slaves to a free people, to forge a new future.
The situation could not have gotten much worse just before their deliverance.
Remember this: Jesus at his crucifixion, the worst day of his life, took a thief to Glory
Your change has arrived, right now, in the midst of your troubles.
Moses was charged, he was challenged, and then millions of people were changed.
If Jesus is the author and finisher of our faith, that means our futures can be changed in a moment's time!

"ALTERNATIVES"

"And if it seem evil unto you to serve the lord, choose you this day whom ye will serve; whether the gods which your fathers served that were on the other side of the flood, or the gods of the Amorites, in whose land ye dwell: but as for me and my house, we will serve the Lord" (Joshua 24:15).

There is always an option.

Choice is a powerful human capability. Use it wisely.

"THE BLESSINGS"

Changers learn and then teach. A great life lesson reward is to see the blessing in the middle of mayhem.

One of the first words of advice my doctor had for me when my journey with cancer began was the fact that my hair would simply fall out. Yet, another challenge added to the horrendous events unfolding in my life. I always thought, *Lord I don't mind my hair turning grey, but please don't let it turn loose.* I was halfway through the radiation and chemotherapy when my wife and I noticed the blessing: I still had my hair. When all was said and done, I never lost my hair. I had no side-burns, but that was the style then.

"SEND OUT JUDAH"

Change is a choice.

Jesus said, "If I be lifted up, I will draw all men unto me" (John 12:32). He was lifted once by a cross. Now, we are the ones that must see to it that he is lifted up in praise.

Judah defined means praise.

"Some *trust* in chariots, and some in horses but we will remember the name of the *LORD* our God" (Psalms 20:7).

Send in praise, and God will be with you in struggle and mop up the enemy. "And when they began to sing and to praise, the LORD set ambushments against the children of Ammon, Moab, and mount Seir, which were come against Judah; and they were smitten" (2 Chronicles 20:22).

When we send out Judah (praise), our God is elevated in our lives. When he becomes bigger and better than anything against us, he has promised to be our overcomer and conqueror. Choose change and send out your praise to bring down everything that's against you.

As David, you will take down giants. As Joshua, you will bring down walls. As Moses, you will part your problems.

Send out Judah and expend your energy in praise. Root out the doubt with a resounding shout to the God that can walk on water and calm our troubled seas.

When the doctor looked at me as if to say, "You are living on borrowed time," I knew something had to change. When I began singing, "This is how we over come," all alone in that hospital room, something did change. I sent praise ahead of me. God received it and suddenly stepped up and placed himself between me and disease—even death itself.

Send forth praise to recover from your past, send forth praise to sustain you in your present, and send forth praise to secure you in your future.

Every time Israel sent in Judah (praise), God sent an ambush against the enemy.

Praise says to all of our circumstances, *I don't understand why I'm going through this.* To praise, it doesn't matter.

Let praise, not the problem, take precedence.

Offer hallelujahs, not coerced, but voluntarily from your heart.

Watch our God move where we can't move, touch where we can't touch. Bless, strengthen, heal, deliver, and exalt where we cannot.

"The Finale Miracle"

> Today is Thursday June 23rd 6:30 p.m. Kenny said he felt like he had a Charley horse in his neck. He laid down on the bed. I stood over him in shock as I watched his neck on the right side begin to swell instantly. I thought the staples from his last surgery were going to burst out. He was in excruciating pain. I called 911. We are in an ambulance. Siren blaring, high speeds and racing to hospital. Now Kenny is having hard time breathing.
>
> In the ER, the doctor removed the staples from Kenny's incision in his neck. Diagnosis: a stitch that connected a main artery has

broken loose. Blood is pouring everywhere. Clumps of blood are being pulled out of my husband's neck. He's bleeding profusely. I couldn't believe they let me stay. I was holding Kenny's hand and praying and helping to soak up the blood with gauze as it was pouring out. His blood pressure dropped to 81/47.

He was rushed to surgery. They connected him to three IVs. An artery broke loose close to his ear. They placed a breathing tube deep into his throat. He has to be monitored very closely. They would not let me stay with my husband that night. This is the first time I could not be beside him in this horrendous battle with cancer. I called ICU at 4am, Kenny is doing fine.

We finally got to see him as he was being transferred to another area of the hospital. Our son, Carson, was very upset to see his dad like that. Kenny was heavily sedated. The nurse, Diane, told us to talk to Kenny. She said that he could hear us, but he can't move or respond. When Carson started talking to his dad, you could hear in his trembling voice that he was very concerned about him. When

Carson said, "Dad, I love you," Kenny started moving and trying to get up to comfort him. The nurse said "Mr. Marshburn you cannot get up," at the same time she was pumping more meds into him. My husband is a great dad. He could not take the fact that his son was hurting for him. The next day I told him what happened. He did not remember.

Dr. Mims told me it was a good thing I called 911. He said that when I came into the ER that Kenny might have had just thirty minutes to live. He was bleeding out from the broken artery in his neck. A few days later we walked out of the hospital. That was twelve years ago.

Circumstances charged me, my decision challenged me, and my God changed me.

www.ingramcontent.com/pod-product-compliance
Lightning Source LLC
LaVergne TN
LVHW021742060526
838200LV00052B/3432